Oversized Sweaters

LEISURE ARTS, INC. • Maumelle, Arkansas

Who wouldn't love some "Me Time" in a new, comfortable sweater?

Oversized Sweaters is here to fulfill that desire! Soft and swingy fashions will carry the day plus chase the chill at night. Throw one on with your favorite pair of jeans for a "go-to" leisure time outfit. These attractive crochet sweaters are made with either medium or bulky weight yarns, with simple stitches and easy construction. So pick one out to make for next weekend!

contents

striped tunic

●●○○ EASY

shopping list

YARN (Bulky Weight) BULKY 5

[8.8 ounces, 466 yards (250 grams, 426 meters) per skein]:

- ○ Color A (Off White) - 1{2-2-2} skein(s)
- ○ Color B (Grey) - 1{2-2-2} skein(s)

CROCHET HOOK

- ○ Size L (8 mm) **or** size needed for gauge

ADDITIONAL SUPPLIES

- ○ Yarn needle

size info

FINISHED BUST MEASUREMENT:

{37-41}{45-49-53}"/
{94-104}{114.5-124.5-134.5} cm

FINISHED LENGTH:

27" (68.5 cm)

SIZE NOTE:

We have printed the instructions for the sizes in different colors to make it easier for you to find:

- size Small in Blue
- size Medium in Pink
- size Large in Green
- size 1X in Red
- size 2X in Navy

Instructions in Black apply to all sizes.

gauge info

In pattern, 3 V-Sts and 4 rows = 3" (7.5 cm)

GAUGE SWATCH:

3½" wide x 3" high (9 cm x 7.5 cm)
With Color A, ch 13.
Work same as Back, page 6, for 4 rows: 3 V-Sts.
Finish off.

stitch guide

V-STITCH *(abbreviated V-St)*

(Dc, ch 1, dc) in st or sp indicated.

Entire Tunic is made by alternating 2 rows **each** of Color A and Color B. Do **not** cut yarn until instructed, carry unused yarn loosely along the edge.

BODY

With Color A, ch {58-64}{70-76-82}.

Row 1 (Right side)**:** Work V-St in fifth ch from hook **(4 skipped chs count as first dc plus one skipped ch)**, (skip next 2 chs, work V-St in next ch) across to last 2 chs, skip next ch, dc in last ch: {18-20}{22-24-26} V-Sts.

Note: Loop a short piece of yarn around any stitch to mark Row 1 as **right** side.

Row 2: Ch 3 **(counts as first dc, now and throughout)**, turn; work V-St in each V-St (ch-1 sp) across, dc in last dc changing to Color B ***(Fig. A)***; do **not** cut yarn.

Row 3: Ch 3, turn; work V-St in each V-St across, dc in last dc.

Row 4: Ch 3, turn; work V-St in each V-St across, dc in last dc changing colors.

Repeat Rows 3 and 4 for pattern until piece measures approximately 25½" (65 cm) from beginning ch, ending by working a **wrong** side row.

Fig. A

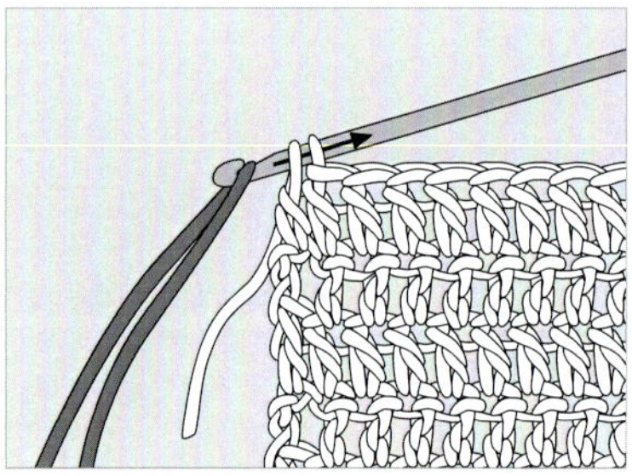

NECK SHAPING

FIRST SIDE

Row 1: Ch 3, turn; work V-St in next {5-6}{7-8-9} V-Sts, dc in first dc of next V-St, leave remaining sts unworked.

Row 2: Ch 3, turn; work V-St in each V-St across, dc in last dc; finish off.

SECOND SIDE

Row 1: With **right** side facing and using the same color used for First Side, skip next 8 ch-1 sps from First Side and join yarn with slip st in next dc; ch 3, work V-St in each V-St across, dc in last dc: {5-6}{7-8-9} V-Sts.

Row 2: Ch 3, turn; work V-St in each V-St across, dc in last dc; finish off.

front

Work same as Back until piece measures 2 rows less than Back to Neck Shaping, ending by working a **wrong** side row.

NECK SHAPING

FIRST SIDE

Row 1: Ch 3, turn; work {5-6} {7-8-9} V-Sts, dc in first dc of next V-St, leave remaining sts unworked.

Row 2: Ch 3, turn; work V-St in each V-St across, dc in last dc changing colors.

Rows 3 and 4: Ch 3, turn; work V-St in each V-St across, dc in last dc.

Finish off.

SECOND SIDE

Row 1: With **right** side facing and using the same color used for First Side, skip next 8 ch-1 sps from First Side and join yarn with slip st in next dc; ch 3, work V-St in each V-St across, dc in last dc: {5-6} {7-8-9} V-Sts.

Complete same as First Side.

sleeve (make 2)

With Color A, ch {52-58}{58-64-64}.

Work same as Back until Sleeve measures approximately {19-18½}{17½-16½-16}"/{48.5-47} {44.5-42-40.5} cm from beginning ch: {16-18}{18-20-20} V-Sts.

Finish off.

finishing

Whipstitch the shoulder seams *(Figs. 1a & b, page 43)*.

Beginning and ending {8¼-9¼} {9¼-10¼-10¼}"/{21-23.5} {23.5-26-26} cm down from shoulder seam, whipstitch last row of Sleeves to piece, matching center of last row on Sleeve to shoulder seam.

Beginning at Sleeve edge, whipstitch underarm and side in one continuous seam, leaving last 5" (12.5 cm) open.

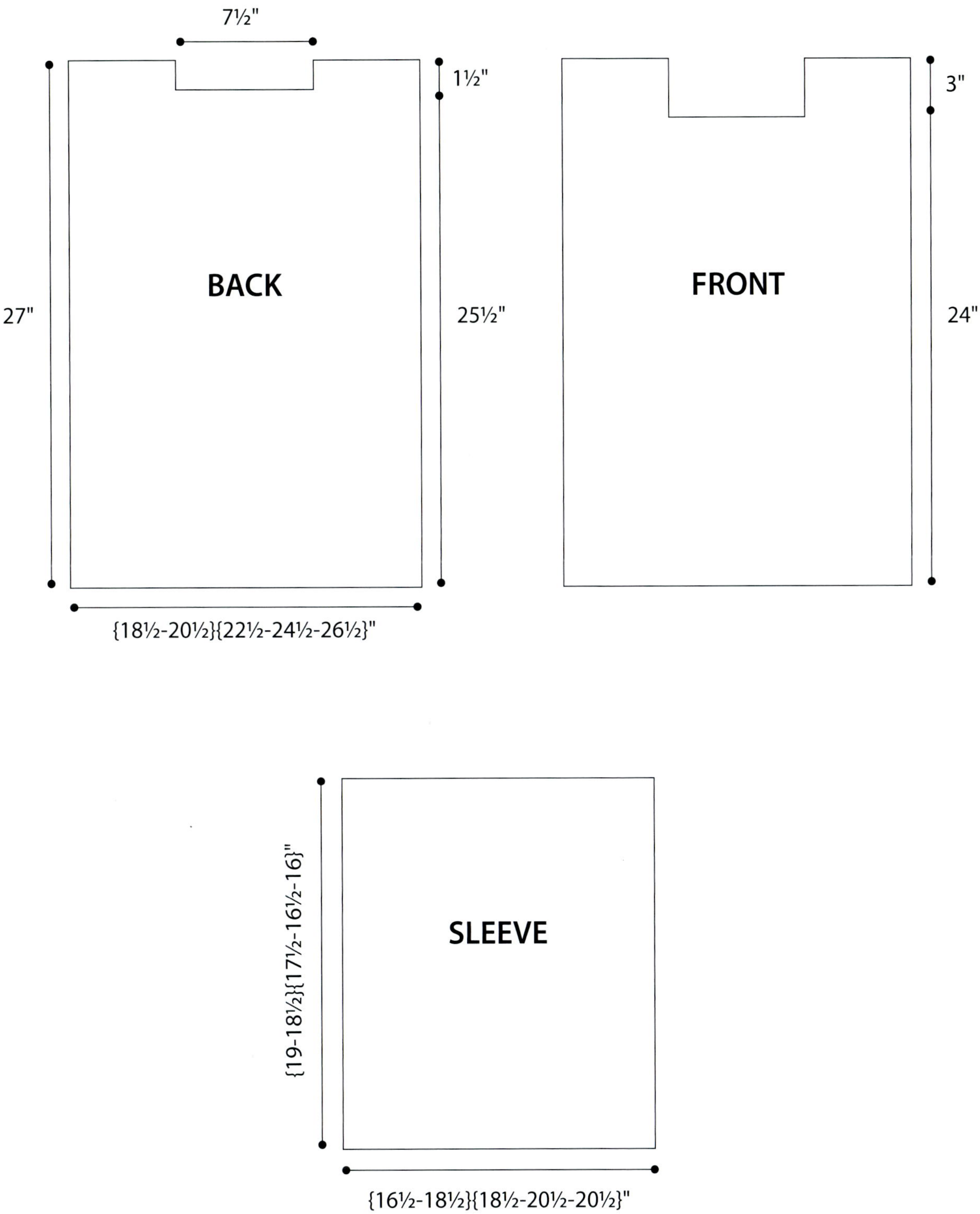
7½"
1½"
BACK
27"
25½"
{18½-20½}{22½-24½-26½}"
3"
FRONT
24"
SLEEVE
{19-18½}{17½-16½-16}"
{16½-18½}{18½-20½-20½}"

misty hoodie

●●○○ EASY

shopping list

YARN (Medium Weight) MEDIUM 4

[3.5 ounces, 270 yards (100 grams, 247 meters) per skein]:

○ {8-9}{9-10-10} skeins

CROCHET HOOK

○ Size K (6.5 mm) **or** size needed for gauge

ADDITIONAL SUPPLIES

○ Yarn needle

size info

FINISHED BUST MEASUREMENT:

{36½-40}{44½-48-52½}"/

{92.5-101.5}{113-122-133.5} cm

FINISHED LENGTH:

{29-29½}{29½-30-30½}"/

{73.5-75}{75-76-77.5} cm

SIZE NOTE:

We have printed the instructions for the sizes in different colors to make it easier for you to find:

- size Small in Blue
- size Medium in Pink
- size Large in Green
- size 1X in Red
- size 2X in Navy

Instructions in Black apply to all sizes.

gauge info

In pattern, 14 sts and 14 rows = 4" (10 cm)

GAUGE SWATCH: 4" (10 cm) square

Ch 15.

Work same as Back, page 12, for 14 rows: 14 sts.

Finish off.

stitch guide

SC/DC 2 TOGETHER ***(abbreviated sc/dc2tog)***

(uses next dc and next sc)

Pull up a loop in **next** dc, YO, insert hook in **next** sc, YO and pull up a loop (4 loops on hook), YO and draw through 3 loops on hook, YO and draw through both loops on hook **(counts as one st)**.

DC/SC 2 TOGETHER ***(abbreviated dc/sc2tog)***

(uses next sc and next dc)

YO, insert hook in **next** sc, YO and pull up a loop (3 loops on hook), YO and draw through 2 loops on hook, pull up a loop in **next** dc, YO and draw through all 3 loops on hook **(counts as one st)**.

back

BODY

Ch {65-71}{79-85-93}.

Row 1 (Right side)**:** Sc in third ch from hook **(2 skipped chs count as first hdc, now and throughout)**, dc in next ch, (sc in next ch, dc in next ch) across to last ch, hdc in last ch: {64-70}{78-84-92} sts.

Note: Loop a short piece of yarn around any stitch to mark Row 1 as **right** side.

Row 2: Ch 2 **(counts as first hdc, now and throughout)**, turn; (sc in next dc, dc in next sc) across to last hdc, hdc in last hdc.

Repeat Row 2 for pattern until piece measures approximately 20½" (52 cm) from beginning ch, ending by working a **wrong** side row; do **not** finish off.

ARMHOLE SHAPING

Row 1: Slip st in first {7-9}{11-13-15} sts, ch 2, (sc in next dc, dc in next sc) across to last {7-9}{11-13-15} sts, hdc in next dc, leave remaining {6-8}{10-12-14} sts unworked: {52-54}{58-60-64} sts.

Work even until piece measures approximately {29-29½}{29½-30-30½}"/{73.5-75}{75-76-77.5} cm from beginning ch.

Finish off.

pocket lining (make 2)

Row 1 (Right side)**:** Ch 23; hdc in third ch from hook and in each ch across: 22 hdc.

Note: Mark Row 1 as **right** side.

pocket lining

Row 2: Ch 2, turn; hdc in next hdc and in each hdc across.

Repeat Row 2 until piece measures approximately 6" (15 cm) from beginning ch, ending by working a **wrong** side row.

Finish off.

left front

BODY

Ch {37-39}{43-47-51}.

Work same as Back until piece measures approximately 7" (18 cm) from beginning ch, ending by working a **wrong** side row: {36-38}{42-46-50} sts.

Place Pocket Lining: Ch 2, turn; maintaining established pattern, work across next {6-7}{9-11-13} sts; holding **right** side of one Pocket Lining **behind** Front, work across 22 hdc on last row of Pocket Lining; skip next 22 sts on Front, work across.

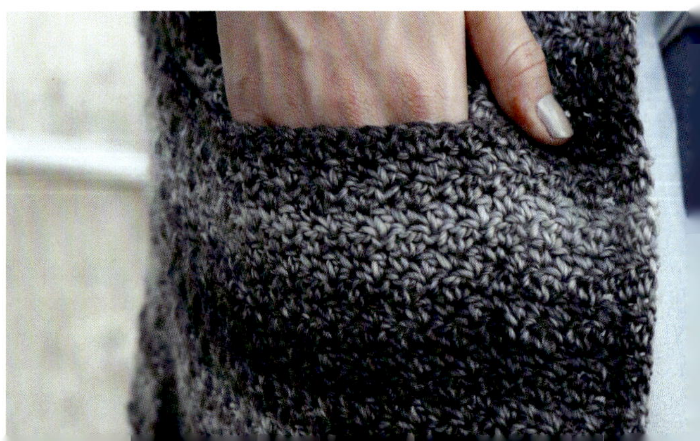

Work even until piece measures approximately 20½" (52 cm) from beginning ch, ending by working a **wrong** side row; do **not** finish off.

ARMHOLE SHAPING

Row 1: Turn; slip st in first {7-9}{11-13-15} sts, ch 2, (sc in next dc, dc in next sc) across to last hdc, hdc in last hdc: {30-30}{32-34-36} sts.

Work even until piece measures approximately {25-25½}{25½-26-26½}"/{63.5-65}{65-66-67.5} cm from beginning ch, ending by working a **right** side row.

NECK SHAPING

Row 1: Turn; slip st in first 9 sts, ch 2, (sc in next dc, dc in next sc) across to last hdc, hdc in last hdc: {22-22}{24-26-28} sts.

Row 2 (Decrease row)**:** Ch 2, turn; (sc in next dc, dc in next sc) across to last 3 sts, sc/dc2tog, hdc in last hdc: {21-21}{23-25-27} sts.

Row 3 (Decrease row)**:** Ch 2, turn; dc/sc2tog, dc in next sc, (sc in next dc, dc in next sc) across to last hdc, hdc in last hdc: {20-20}{22-24-26} sts.

Rows 4-6: Repeat Rows 2 and 3 once, then repeat Row 2 once **more**: {17-17}{19-21-23} sts.

Row 7: Ch 2, turn; dc in next st, (sc in next dc, dc in next sc) across to last hdc, hdc in last hdc.

Row 8 (Decrease row)**:** Ch 2, turn; sc in next dc, (dc in next sc, sc in next dc) across to last 3 sts, dc/sc2tog, hdc in last hdc: {16-16}{18-20-22} sts.

Row 9: Ch 2, turn; (sc in next st, dc in next sc) across to last hdc, hdc in last hdc.

Row 10: Repeat Row 2: {15-15}{17-19-21} sts.

Rows 11 and 12: Repeat Rows 7 and 8: {14-14}{16-18-20} sts.

Work even until Left Front measures same as Back.

Finish off leaving a long end for sewing.

right front

BODY

Work same as Left Front to Armhole Shaping, ending by working a **right** side row; do **not** finish off: {36-38}{42-46-50} sts.

ARMHOLE SHAPING

Work same as Left Front to Neck Shaping, ending by working a **wrong** side row: {30-30}{32-34-36} sts.

NECK SHAPING

Work same as Left Front: {14-14}{16-18-20} sts.

sleeve (make 2)

Ch 35.

Row 1 (Right side)**:** Sc in third ch from hook, dc in next ch, (sc in next ch, dc in next ch) across to last ch, hdc in last ch: 34 sts.

Note: Mark Row 1 as **right** side.

Row 2: Ch 2, turn; (sc in next dc, dc in next sc) across to last hdc, hdc in last hdc.

Increase Row: Ch 2, turn; hdc in first hdc, (sc in next dc, dc in next sc) across to last hdc, 2 hdc in last hdc: 36 sts.

sleeve

Maintaining established pattern and working sts into pattern as they are added, continue to increase one st at each edge, every other row, {0-0}{0-2-7} times ***(see Zeros, page 42)***; then increase every fourth row, {4-11}{13-13-10} times; then increase every sixth row, {8-3}{1-0-0} time(s): {60-64}{64-66-70} sts.

Work even until Sleeve measures approximately {21½-21½}{21-20½-20½}"/{54.5-54.5}{53.5-52-52} cm from beginning ch.

Finish off.

finishing

Whipstitch the shoulder seams across {14-14}{16-18-20} sts ***(Figs. 1a & b, page 43)***, leaving center {24-26}{26-24-24} sts unsewn.

HOOD

Row 1: With **right** side facing, join yarn with slip st in first st on Right Front Neck Shaping; ch 1, work 22 sc evenly spaced across to shoulder, sc in each st across Back neck, work 22 sc evenly spaced across Left Front Neck Shaping: {68-70}{70-68-68} sc.

finishing

Row 2: Ch 2, turn; (sc in next st, dc in next st) across to last st, hdc in last st.

Repeat Row 2 for pattern until Hood measures approximately 12" (30.5 cm).

Finish off leaving a long end for sewing.

Fold the last row of Hood in half with **wrong** side together; whipstitch across row to form top of Hood.

Place a marker at each edge of Sleeve, {1¾-2¼}{3-3½-4}"/{4.5-5.5}{7.5-9-10} cm down from last row for seam placement. Place a marker at center of last row.

Matching center of last row on Sleeve to shoulder seam, whipstitch top of Sleeve to Armhole edge; sew Armhole Shaping to marker on each side of Sleeve.

Whipstitch underarm and side in one continuous seam.

Sew the Pocket Linings to the **wrong** side of Fronts.

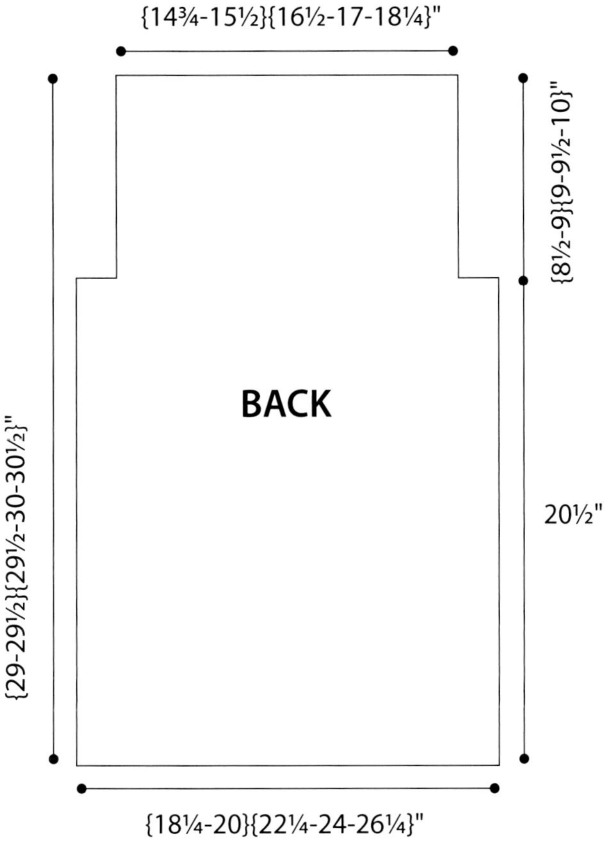
{14¾-15½}{16½-17-18¼}"
{8½-9}{9-9½-10}"
BACK
{29-29½}{29½-30-30½}"
20½"
{18¼-20}{22¼-24-26¼}"

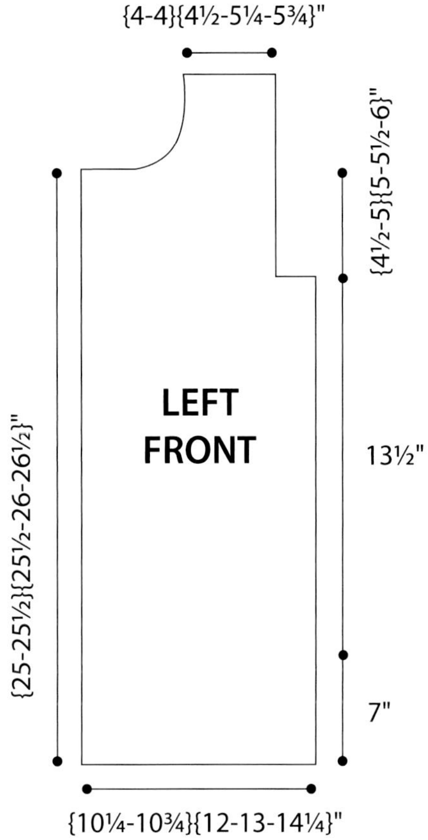
{4-4}{4½-5¼-5¾}"
{4½-5}{5-5½-6}"
LEFT FRONT
{25-25½}{25½-26-26½}"
13½"
7"
{10¼-10¾}{12-13-14¼}"

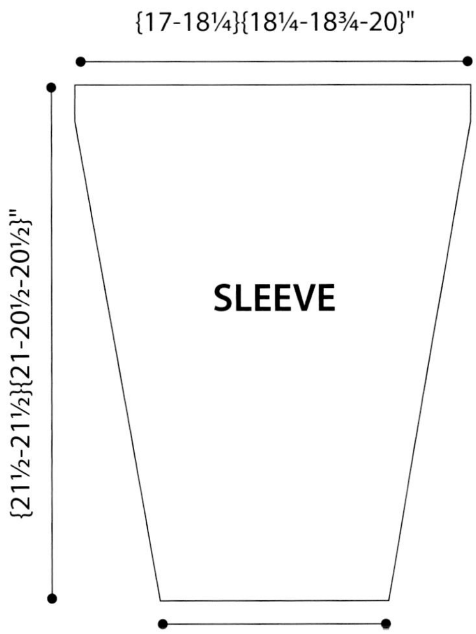
{17-18¼}{18¼-18¾-20}"
SLEEVE
{21½-21½}{21-20½-20½}"
9¾"

black & strappy

●●○○ EASY

shopping list

YARN (Bulky Weight) BULKY 5

[3.5 ounces, 127 yards (100 grams, 116 meters) per skein**]**:

○ {9-10}{10-11-11} skeins

CROCHET HOOK

○ Size L (8 mm) **or** size needed for gauge

ADDITIONAL SUPPLIES

○ Yarn needle

size info

FINISHED BUST MEASUREMENT:

{39-42¾}{46¼-49¾-53¼}"/

{99-108.5}{117.5-126.5-135.5} cm

FINISHED LENGTH:

{26-26½}{26½-27-27}"/

{66-67.5}{67.5-68.5-68.5} cm

SIZE NOTE:

We have printed the instructions for the sizes in different colors to make it easier for you to find:

- size Small in Blue
- size Medium in Pink
- size Large in Green
- size 1X in Red
- size 2X in Navy

Instructions in Black apply to all sizes.

gauge info

In pattern, 9 sts and 9 rows = 4" (10 cm)

GAUGE SWATCH:

4½" wide x 4" high (11.5 cm x 10 cm)

Ch 11.

Work same as Front, page 18, for 9 rows: 10 sts.

Finish off.

stitch guide

SC/DC 2 TOGETHER ***(abbreviated sc/dc2tog)***

(uses next dc and next sc)

Pull up a loop in **next** dc, YO, insert hook in **next** sc, YO and pull up a loop (4 loops on hook), YO and draw through 3 loops on hook, YO and draw through both loops on hook **(counts as one st)**.

DC/SC 2 TOGETHER ***(abbreviated dc/sc2tog)***

(uses next sc and next dc)

YO, insert hook in **next** sc, YO and pull up a loop (3 loops on hook), YO and draw through 2 loops on hook, pull up a loop in **next** dc, YO and draw through all 3 loops on hook **(counts as one st)**.

BODY

Ch {45-49}{53-57-61}.

Row 1 (Right side)**:** Sc in third ch from hook **(2 skipped chs count as first hdc, now and throughout)**, dc in next ch, (sc in next ch, dc in next ch) across to last ch, hdc in last ch: {44-48}{52-56-60} sts.

Note: Loop a short piece of yarn around any stitch to mark Row 1 as **right** side.

Row 2: Ch 2 **(counts as first hdc, now and throughout)**, turn; (sc in next dc, dc in next sc) across to last hdc, hdc in last hdc.

Repeat Row 2 for pattern until piece measures approximately 17½" (44.5 cm) from beginning ch, ending by working a **wrong** side row; do **not** finish off.

SLEEVE SHAPING

Row 1: Ch {45-43}{41-39-37}, turn; sc in third ch from hook, dc in next ch, (sc in next st, dc in next st) across to last hdc, hdc in last hdc: {88-90}{92-94-96} sts.

Row 2: Repeat Row 1: 132 sts.

Work even until piece measures approximately {23-23½}{23½-24-24}"/{58.5-59.5}{59.5-61-61} cm from beginning ch, ending by working a **wrong** side row.

NECK SHAPING

FIRST SIDE

Row 1: Ch 2, turn; (sc in next dc, dc in next sc) 30 times, hdc in next dc, leave remaining 70 sts unworked: 62 sts.

Row 2: Ch 2, turn; sc/dc2tog, (sc in next dc, dc in next sc) across to last hdc, hdc in last hdc: 61 sts.

Row 3: Ch 2, turn; sc in next dc, (dc in next sc, sc in next dc) across to last 3 sts, dc/sc2tog, hdc in last hdc: 60 sts.

Row 4: Ch 2, turn; (sc in next st, dc in next sc) across to last hdc, hdc in last hdc.

Row 5: Ch 2, turn; (sc in next dc, dc in next sc) across to last 3 sts, sc/dc2tog, hdc in last hdc: 59 sts.

Row 6: Ch 2, turn; dc in next st, (sc in next dc, dc in next sc) across to last hdc, hdc in last hdc.

Row 7: Ch 2, turn; sc in next dc, (dc in next sc, sc in next dc) across to last 3 sts, dc/sc2tog, hdc in last hdc; finish off: 58 sts.

front

SECOND SIDE

Row 1: With **right** side facing, skip next 8 sts from First Side and join yarn with slip st in next sc; ch 2, (sc in next dc, dc in next sc) across to last hdc, hdc in last hdc: 62 sts.

Row 2: Ch 2, turn; (sc in next dc, dc in next sc) across to last 3 sts, sc/dc2tog, hdc in last hdc: 61 sts.

Row 3: Ch 2, turn; dc/sc2tog, dc in next sc, (sc in next dc, dc in next sc) across to last hdc, hdc in last hdc: 60 sts.

Row 4: Ch 2, turn; (sc in next dc, dc in next st) across to last hdc, hdc in last hdc.

Row 5: Ch 2, turn; sc/dc2tog, (sc in next dc, dc in next sc) across to last hdc, hdc in last hdc: 59 sts.

Row 6: Ch 2, turn; sc in next dc, (dc in next sc, sc in next st) across to last hdc, hdc in last hdc.

Row 7: Ch 2, turn; dc/sc2tog, dc in next sc, (sc in next dc, dc in next sc) across to last hdc, hdc in last hdc; finish off: 58 sts.

back

Work same as Front until piece measures approximately {20-20½}{20½-21-21}"/{51-52}{52-53.5-53.5} cm from beginning ch, ending by working a **wrong** side row.

NECK SHAPING

FIRST SIDE

Work same as Front; at end of Row 7, do **not** finish off: 58 sts.

Row 8: Ch 2, turn; (sc in next st, dc in next st) across to last hdc, hdc in last hdc.

back

Repeat Row 8 for pattern until Sleeve measures same as Front.

Finish off.

SECOND SIDE

Work same as Front; at end of Row 7, do **not** finish off: 58 sts.

Complete same as First Side on Back.

finishing

STRAP

Ch 15, slip st in second ch from hook and in each ch across; finish off.

Sew the ends of the Strap to the top of Back Neck Shaping.

Whipstitch shoulder seams and top of Sleeve *(Figs. 1a & b, page 43)*.

Whipstitch underarm and side in one continuous seam.

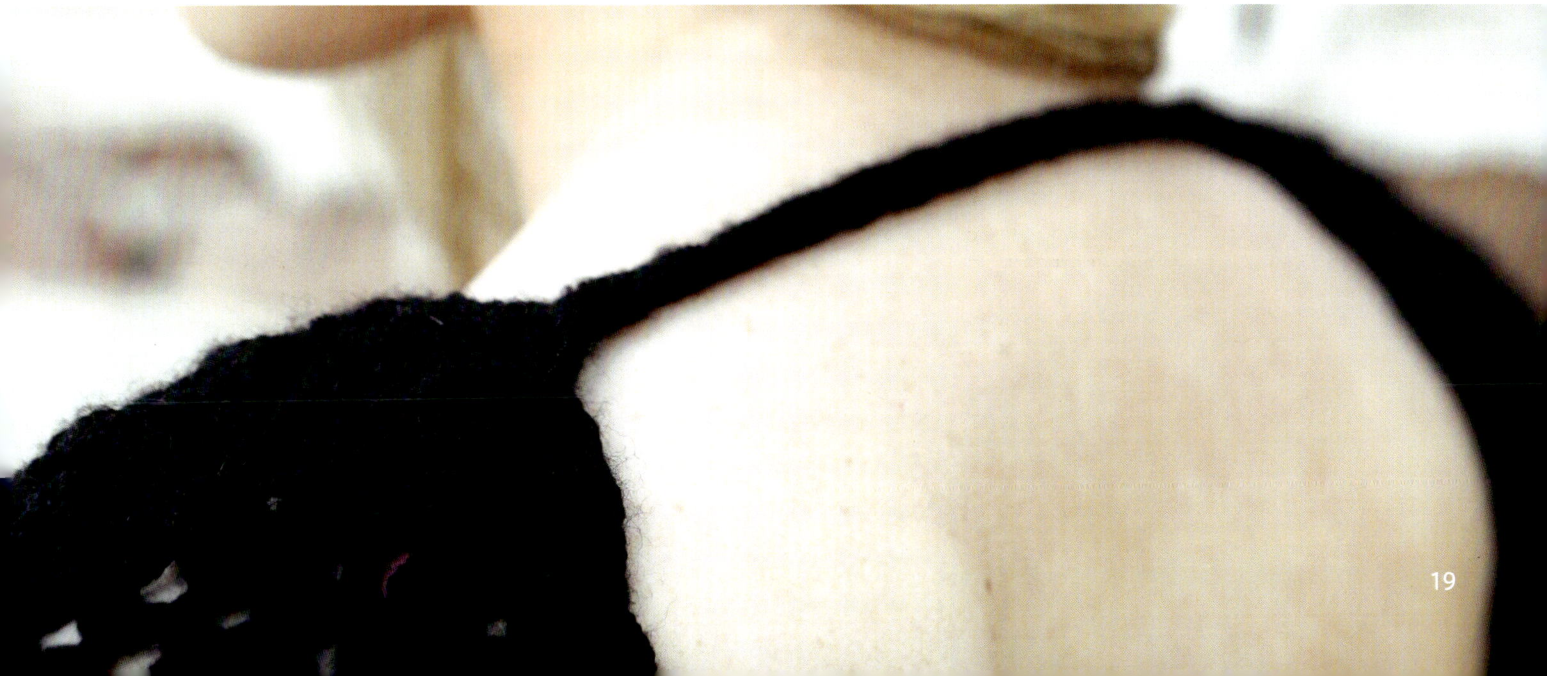

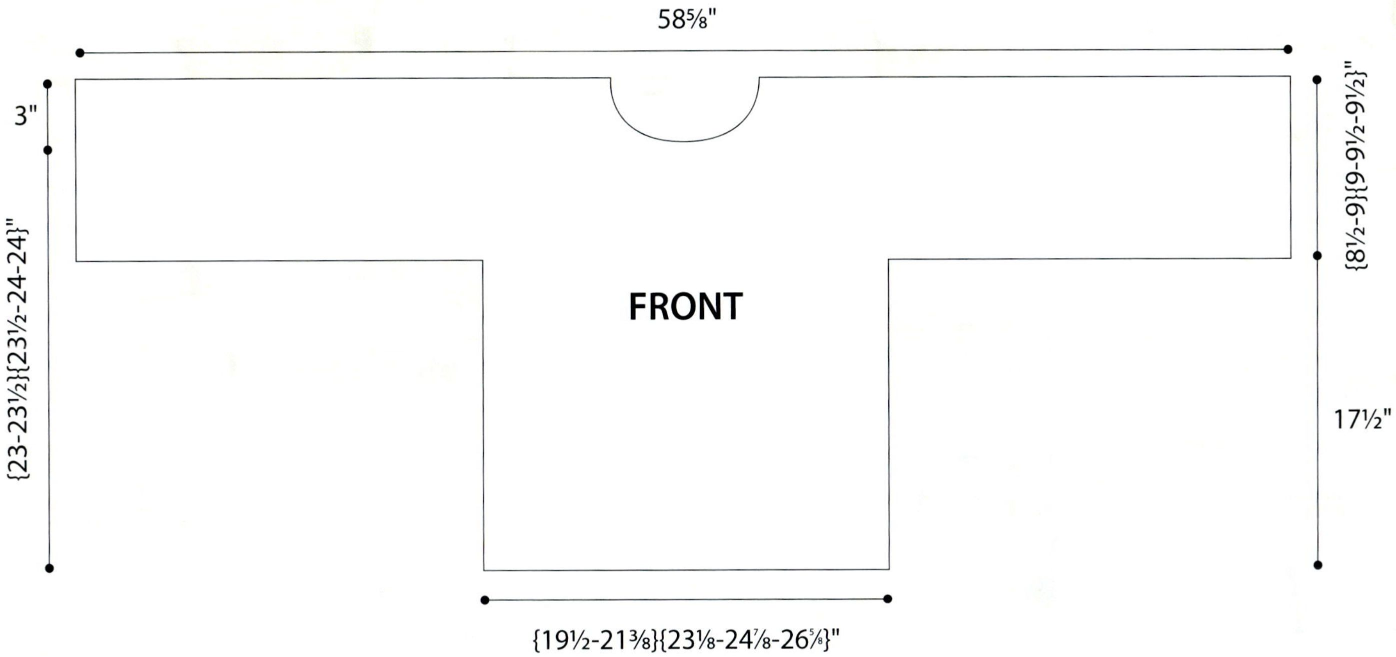
58⅝"
3"
{23-23½}{23½-24-24}"
{8½-9}{9-9½-9½}"
17½"
FRONT
{19½-21⅜}{23⅛-24⅞-26⅝}"

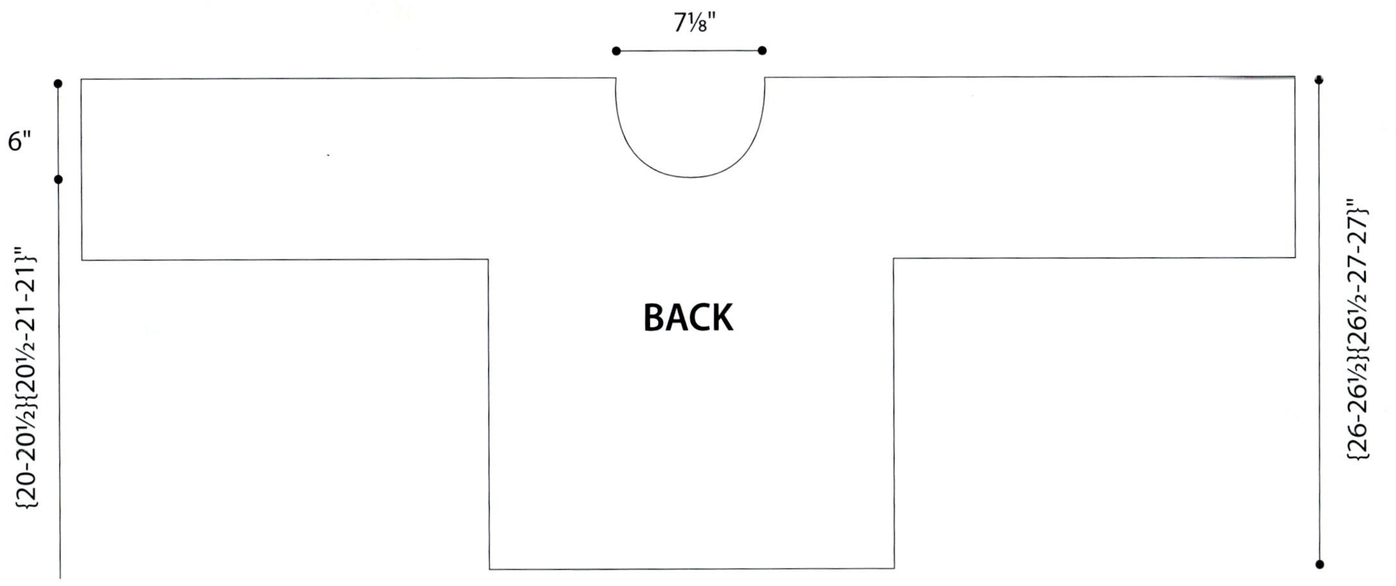
7⅛"
6"
{20-20½}{20½-21-21}"
{26-26½}{26½-27-27}"
BACK

SIZE NOTE:

We have printed the instructions for the sizes in different colors to make it easier for you to find:

- size Small in Blue
- size Medium in Pink
- size Large in Green
- size 1X in Red
- size 2X in Navy

Instructions in Black apply to all sizes.

slouchy pullover ●●○○ EASY

shopping list

YARN (Medium Weight) MEDIUM 4

[3.5 ounces, 246 yards (100 grams, 225 meters) per skein**]**:

○ {7-7}{8-8-9} skeins

CROCHET HOOK

○ Size J (6 mm) **or** size needed for gauge

ADDITIONAL SUPPLIES

○ Yarn needle

size info

FINISHED BUST MEASUREMENT:

{38½-42½}{46½-50½-54¾}"/

{98-108}{118-128.5-139} cm

FINISHED LENGTH:

26" (66 cm)

gauge info

In pattern, 12 sts and 12 rows = 4" (10 cm)

GAUGE SWATCH: 4" (10 cm) square

Ch 13.

Work same as Back, page 24, for 12 rows: 12 sts.

Finish off.

stitch guide

SC/DC 2 TOGETHER ***(abbreviated sc/dc2tog)***

(uses next dc and next sc)

Pull up a loop in **next** dc, YO, insert hook in **next** sc, YO and pull up a loop (4 loops on hook), YO and draw through 3 loops on hook, YO and draw through both loops on hook **(counts as one st)**.

DC/SC 2 TOGETHER ***(abbreviated dc/sc2tog)***

(uses next sc and next dc)

YO, insert hook in **next** sc, YO and pull up a loop (3 loops on hook), YO and draw through 2 loops on hook, pull up a loop in **next** dc, YO and draw through all 3 loops on hook **(counts as one st)**.

FRONT POST DOUBLE CROCHET

(abbreviated FPdc)

YO, insert hook from **front** to **back** around post of st indicated ***(Fig. A)***, YO and pull up a loop (3 loops on hook), (YO and draw through 2 loops on hook) twice.

BACK POST DOUBLE CROCHET

(abbreviated BPdc)

YO, insert hook from **back** to **front** around post of st indicated ***(Fig. A)***, YO and pull up a loop (3 loops on hook), (YO and draw through 2 loops on hook) twice.

Fig. A

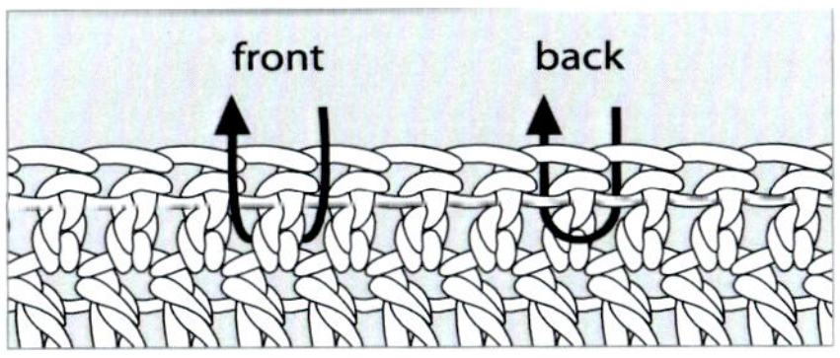

BODY

Ch {59-65}{71-77-83}.

Row 1 (Right side)**:** Sc in third ch from hook **(2 skipped chs count as first hdc, now and throughout)**, dc in next ch, (sc in next ch, dc in next ch) across to last ch, hdc in last ch: {58-64}{70-76-82} sts.

Note: Loop a short piece of yarn around any stitch to mark Row 1 as **right** side.

Row 2: Ch 2 **(counts as first hdc, now and throughout)**, turn; (sc in next dc, dc in next sc) across to last hdc, hdc in last hdc.

Repeat Row 2 for pattern until piece measures approximately {17-17}{16½-16½-16}"/{43-43}{42-42-40.5} cm from beginning ch, ending by working a **wrong** side row; do **not** finish off.

ARMHOLE SHAPING

Row 1: Turn; slip st in first {5-5}{7-7-7} sts, ch 2, (sc in next dc, dc in next sc) across to last {5-5}{7-7-7} sts, hdc in next dc, leave remaining {4-4}{6-6-6} sts unworked: {50-56}{58-64-70} sts.

Work even until piece measures approximately 23" (58.5 cm) from beginning ch, ending by working a **wrong** side row.

NECK SHAPING

Maintain established pattern throughout.

FIRST SIDE

Row 1: Ch 2, turn; (sc in next dc, dc in next sc) {9-10}{11-12-13} times, hdc in next dc, leave remaining {30-34}{34-38-42} sts unworked: {20-22}{24-26-28} sts.

Row 2: Ch 2, turn; sc/dc2tog, (sc in next dc, dc in next sc) across to last hdc, hdc in last hdc: {19-21}{23-25-27} sts.

Row 3: Ch 2, turn; (sc in next dc, dc in next sc) across to last 3 sts, dc/sc2tog, hdc in last hdc: {18-20}{22-24-26} sts.

Row 4 (Decrease row)**:** Ch 2, turn; sc/dc2tog, (sc in next dc, dc in next sc) across to last hdc, hdc in last hdc: {17-19}{21-23-25} sts.

Row 5: Ch 2, turn; sc in next dc, (dc in next sc, sc in next dc) across to last hdc, hdc in last hdc.

Row 6: Ch 2, turn; dc/sc2tog, dc in next sc, (sc in next dc, dc in next sc) across to last hdc, hdc in last hdc: {16-18}{20-22-24} sts.

Row 7: Ch 2, turn; (sc in next dc, dc in next sc) across to last hdc, hdc in last hdc.

Row 8: Repeat Row 4: {15-17}{19-21-23} sts.

Row 9: Ch 2, turn; sc in next dc, (dc in next sc, sc in next dc) across to last hdc, hdc in last hdc; finish off.

SECOND SIDE

Row 1: With **right** side facing, skip next {10-12}{10-12-14} sts from First Side and join yarn with slip st in next st; ch 2, (sc in next dc, dc in next sc) across to last hdc, hdc in last hdc: {20-22}{24-26-28} sts.

Row 2: Ch 2, turn; (sc in next dc, dc in next sc) across to last 3 sts, sc/dc2tog, hdc in last hdc: {19-21}{23-25-27} sts.

Row 3: Ch 2, turn; dc/sc2tog, dc in next sc, (sc in next dc, dc in next sc) across to last 3 sts, hdc in last hdc: {18-20}{22-24-26} sts.

Row 4 (Decrease row)**:** Ch 2, turn; (sc in next dc, dc in next sc) across to last 3 sts, sc/dc2tog, hdc in last hdc: {17-19}{21-23-25} sts.

Row 5: Ch 2, turn; dc in next st, (sc in next dc, dc in next sc) across to last hdc, hdc in last hdc.

Row 6: Ch 2, turn; sc in next dc, (dc in next sc, sc in next dc) across to last 3 sts, dc/sc2tog, hdc in last hdc: {16-18}{20-22-24} sts.

Row 7: Ch 2, turn; (sc in next dc, dc in next sc) across to last hdc, hdc in last hdc.

Row 8: Repeat Row 4: {15-17}{19-21-23} sts.

Row 9: Ch 2, turn; dc in next sc, (sc in next dc, dc in next sc) across to last hdc, hdc in last hdc; finish off.

front

Work same as Back.

sleeve (make 2)

Ch 47.

Row 1 (Right side)**:** Sc in third ch from hook, dc in next ch, (sc in next ch, dc in next ch) across to last ch, hdc in last ch: 46 sts.

Note: Mark Row 1 as **right** side.

Rows 2-6: Ch 2, turn; (sc in next dc, dc in next sc) across to last hdc, hdc in last hdc.

Increase Row: Ch 2, turn; hdc in first hdc, (sc in next dc, dc in next sc) across to last hdc, 2 hdc in last hdc: 48 sts.

Maintaining established pattern and working sts into pattern as they are added, continue to increase one st at each edge, every sixth row, {0-0}{0-0-7} times ***(see Zeros, page 42)***; then increase every eighth row, {0-0}{3-3-0} times; then increase every tenth row, {0-0}{2-2-0} times; then increase every twelfth row, {4-4}{0-0-0} times: {56-56}{58-58-62} sts.

Work even until Sleeve measures approximately {20-20}{19½-18½-18}"/{51-51}{49.5-47-45.5} cm from beginning ch.

Finish off.

finishing

Whipstitch one shoulder seam ***(Figs. 1a & b, page 43)***.

NECKBAND

With **right** side facing and beginning at unsewn shoulder, join yarn with slip st in end of first row; ch 3, work {57-61}{57-61-65} dc evenly spaced along neckline: {58-62}{58-63-66} sts.

Row 1: Ch 2, turn; (work FPdc around next st, work BPdc around next st) across to last st, hdc in top of turning ch.

Repeat Row 1 until Neckband measures approximately 3½" (9 cm).

Finish off.

Whipstitch second shoulder and Neckband in one continuous seam.

Place a marker at each edge of Sleeve, {1⅜-1⅜}{2-2-2}"/{3.5-3.5}{5-5-5} cm down from last row for seam placement. Place a marker at center of last row.

Matching center of last row on Sleeve to shoulder seam, whipstitch top of Sleeve to Armhole edge; sew Armhole Shaping to marker on each side of Sleeve.

Beginning at Sleeve edge, whipstitch underarm and side in one continuous seam, leaving last 4" (10 cm) open.

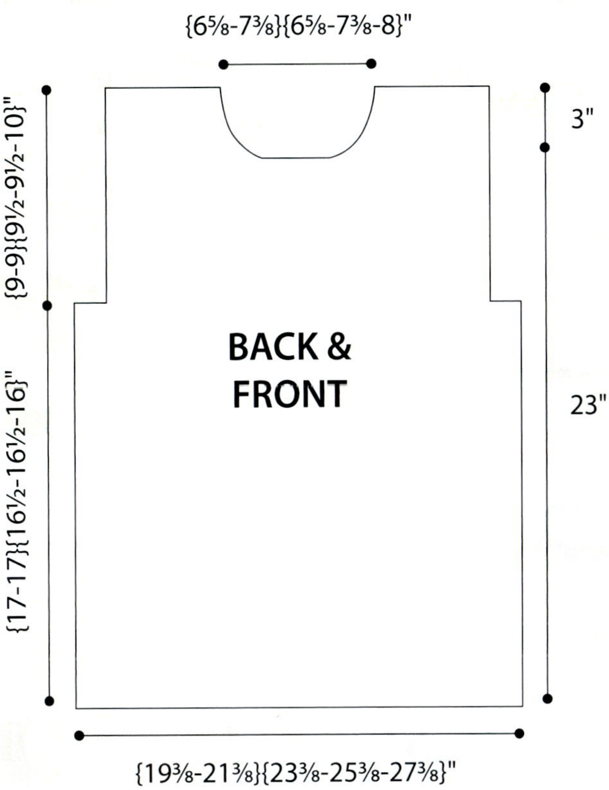
{6⅝-7⅜}{6⅝-7⅜-8}"
{9-9}{9½-9½-10}"
3"
BACK &
FRONT
{17-17}{16½-16½-16}"
23"
{19⅜-21⅜}{23⅜-25⅜-27⅜}"

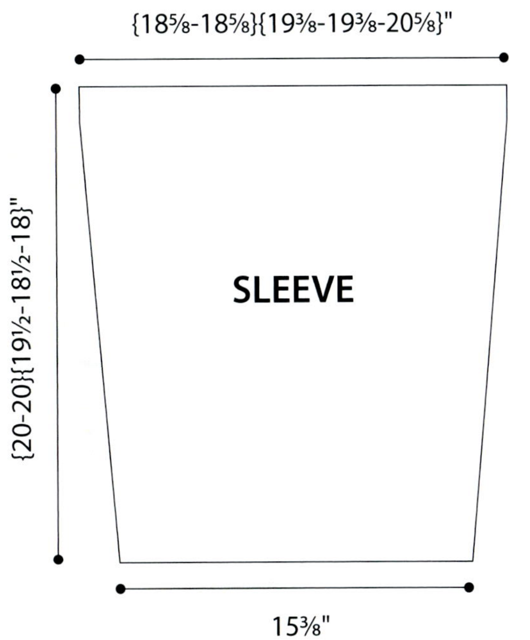
{18⅝-18⅝}{19⅜-19⅜-20⅝}"
{20-20}{19½-18½-18}"
SLEEVE
15⅜"

playful poncho

●●○○ **EASY**

One size fits most

shopping list

YARN (Medium Weight) [MEDIUM 4]

[3.5 ounces, 246 yards (100 grams, 225 meters) per skein**]**:

○ 11 skeins

CROCHET HOOK

○ Size J (6 mm) **or** size needed for gauge

ADDITIONAL SUPPLIES

○ Yarn needle

gauge info

In pattern, 12 sts and 12 rows = 4" (10 cm)

GAUGE SWATCH: 4" (10 cm) square

Ch 13.

Work same as Back, page 30, for 12 rows: 12 sts.

Finish off.

stitch guide

SC/DC 2 TOGETHER ***(abbreviated sc/dc2tog)***

(uses next dc and next sc)

Pull up a loop in **next** dc, YO, insert hook in **next** sc, YO and pull up a loop (4 loops on hook), YO and draw through 3 loops on hook, YO and draw through both loops on hook **(counts as one st)**.

DC/SC 2 TOGETHER ***(abbreviated dc/sc2tog)***

(uses next sc and next dc)

YO, insert hook in **next** sc, YO and pull up a loop (3 loops on hook), YO and draw through 2 loops on hook, pull up a loop in **next** dc, YO and draw through all 3 loops on hook **(counts as one st)**.

Ch 187.

Row 1 (Right side)**:** Sc in third ch from hook **(2 skipped chs count as first hdc)**, dc in next ch, (sc in next ch, dc in next ch) across to last ch, hdc in last ch: 186 sts.

Note: Loop a short piece of yarn around any stitch to mark Row 1 as **right** side.

Row 2: Ch 2 **(counts as first hdc, now and throughout)**, turn; (sc in next dc, dc in next sc) across to last hdc, hdc in last hdc.

Repeat Row 2 for pattern until piece measures approximately 21" (53.5 cm) from beginning ch, ending by working a **wrong** side row; do **not** finish off.

NECK SHAPING

FIRST SIDE

Row 1: Ch 2, turn; (sc in next dc, dc in next sc) 42 times, hdc in next dc, leave remaining 100 sts unworked: 86 sts.

Row 2 (Decrease row)**:** Ch 2, turn; sc/dc2tog, (sc in next dc, dc in next sc) across to last hdc, hdc in last hdc: 85 sts.

Row 3 (Decrease row)**:** Ch 2, turn; sc in next dc, (dc in next sc, sc in next dc) across to last 3 sts, dc/sc2tog, hdc in last hdc: 84 sts.

Rows 4-7: Repeat Rows 2 and 3 twice: 80 sts.

Row 8: Ch 2, turn; (sc in next st, dc in next sc) across to last hdc, hdc in last hdc.

Row 9: Ch 2, turn; (sc in next dc, dc in next sc) across to last 3 sts, sc/dc2tog, hdc in last hdc: 79 sts.

Row 10: Ch 2, turn; dc in next st, (sc in next dc, dc in next sc) across to last hdc, hdc in last hdc.

Row 11: Ch 2, turn; sc in next dc, (dc in next sc, sc in next dc) across to last 3 sts, dc/sc2tog, hdc in last hdc: 78 sts.

Row 12: Ch 2, turn; (sc in next st, dc in next sc) across to last hdc, hdc in last hdc; finish off.

SECOND SIDE

Row 1: With **right** side facing, skip next 14 sts from First Side and join yarn with slip st in next dc; ch 2, dc in next sc, (sc in next dc, dc in next sc) across to last hdc, hdc in last hdc: 86 sts.

Row 2 (Decrease row)**:** Ch 2, turn; sc in next dc, (dc in next sc, sc in next dc) across to last 3 sts, dc/sc2tog, hdc in last hdc: 85 sts.

Row 3 (Decrease row)**:** Ch 2, turn; sc/dc2tog, (sc in next dc, dc in next sc) across to last hdc, hdc in last hdc: 84 sts.

Rows 4-7: Repeat Rows 2 and 3 twice: 80 sts.

Row 8: Ch 2, turn; sc in next dc, (dc in next sc, sc in next st) across to last hdc, hdc in last hdc.

Row 9: Ch 2, turn; dc/sc2tog, dc in next sc, (sc in next dc, dc in next sc) across to last hdc, hdc in last hdc: 79 sts.

Row 10: Ch 2, turn; (sc in next dc, dc in next st) across to last hdc, hdc in last hdc.

Row 11: Ch 2, turn; sc/dc2tog, (sc in next dc, dc in next sc) across to last hdc, hdc in last hdc: 78 sts.

Row 12: Ch 2, turn; sc in next dc, (dc in next sc, sc in next st) across to last hdc, hdc in last hdc; finish off.

front

Work same as Back.

finishing

Whipstitch shoulder seams from Neck edge to last 12 sts ***(Figs. 1a & b, page 43)***; leave last 12 sts unsewn.

NECK EDGING

With **right** side facing, join yarn with slip st at either shoulder seam; ch 1, sc evenly around Neck edge; join with slip st to first sc, finish off.

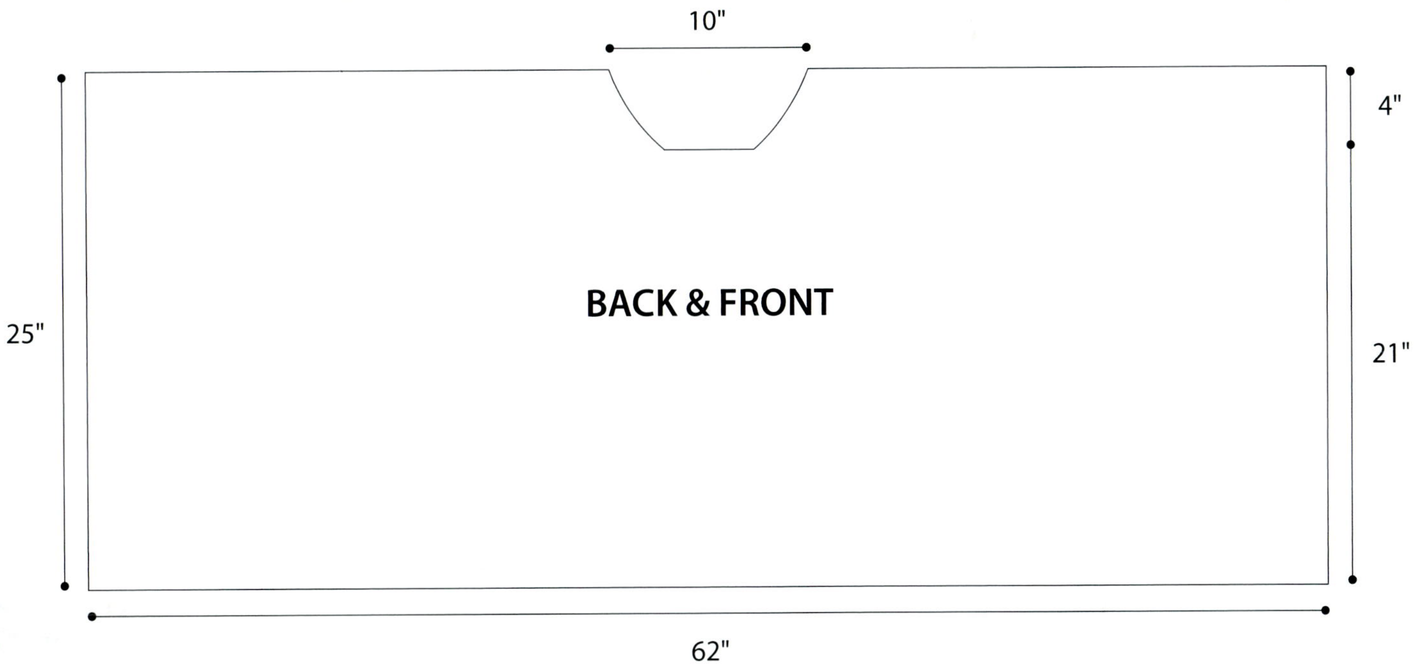
10"
4"
25"
BACK & FRONT
21"
62"

unconstructed jacket

●●○○ EASY

One size fits most

shopping list

YARN (Medium Weight) MEDIUM 4

[3 ounces, 197 yards (85 grams, 180 meters) per skein**]**:

○ 12 skeins

CROCHET HOOK

○ Size L (8 mm) **or** size needed for gauge

ADDITIONAL SUPPLIES

○ Yarn needle

gauge info

In pattern, 9 sts and 9 rows = 4" (10 cm)

GAUGE SWATCH: 4½" (11.5 cm) square

Ch 11.

Work same as Left Front, page 36, for 10 rows: 10 sts.

Finish off.

Jacket is worked from side-to-side in one piece beginning at the Left Front.

Ch 111.

Row 1 (Right side)**:** Sc in third ch from hook **(2 skipped chs count as first hdc, now and throughout)**, dc in next ch, (sc in next ch, dc in next ch) across to last ch, hdc in last ch: 110 sts.

Note: Loop a short piece of yarn around any stitch to mark Row 1 as **right** side.

Row 2: Ch 2 **(counts as first hdc, now and throughout)**, turn; (sc in next dc, dc in next sc) across to last hdc, hdc in last hdc.

Repeat Row 2 for pattern until piece measures approximately 18" (45.5 cm) from beginning ch, ending by working a **wrong** side row; do **not** finish off.

LEFT ARMHOLE SHAPING

FIRST SIDE

(below Armhole opening)

Row 1: Ch 2, turn; (sc in next dc, dc in next sc) 25 times, hdc in next dc, leave remaining 58 sts unworked: 52 sts.

Rows 2-7: Ch 2, turn; (sc in next dc, dc in next sc) across to last hdc, hdc in last hdc.

Place a marker in top of the first hdc on Row 4 to mark underarm.

Finish off.

SECOND SIDE

(above Armhole opening)

Row 1: With **right** side facing, skip next 28 sts from First Side and join yarn with slip st in next sc; ch 2, (sc in next dc, dc in next sc) across to last hdc, hdc in last hdc.

Rows 2-7: Ch 2, turn; (sc in next dc, dc in next sc) across to last hdc, hdc in last hdc; do **not** finish off.

back

Place a marker in top of the last hdc on Row 4 to mark shoulder.

Row 1: Ch 2, turn; sc in next dc, (dc in next sc, sc in next st) across, ch 28, dc in next hdc on First Side, (sc in next dc, dc in next sc) across to last hdc, hdc in last hdc.

Row 2: Ch 2, turn; working in sts and in chs, (sc in next st, dc in next st) across to last hdc, hdc in last hdc.

Work even until piece measures approximately 18" (45.5 cm) from beginning ch of Armhole, ending by working a **wrong** side row; do **not** finish off.

RIGHT ARMHOLE SHAPING

Work same as Left Armhole Shaping.

right front

Row 1: Ch 2, turn; sc in next dc, (dc in next sc, sc in next st) across, ch 28, dc in next hdc on First Side, (sc in next dc, dc in next sc) across to last hdc, hdc in last hdc.

Row 2: Ch 2, turn; working in sts and in chs, (sc in next st, dc in next st) across to last hdc, hdc in last hdc.

right front

Work even until piece measures approximately 18" (45.5 cm) from beginning ch of Armhole, ending by working a **wrong** side row.

Finish off.

sleeve (make 2)

Beginning at wrist, ch 33.

Row 1 (Right side)**:** Sc in third ch from hook, dc in next ch, (sc in next ch, dc in next ch) across to last ch, hdc in last ch: 32 sts.

Note: Mark Row 1 as **right** side.

Row 2: Ch 2, turn; (sc in next dc, dc in next sc) across to last hdc, hdc in last hdc.

Increase Row: Ch 2, turn; hdc in first hdc, (sc in next dc, dc in next sc) across to last hdc, 2 hdc in last hdc: 34 sts.

Maintaining established pattern and working sts into pattern as they are added, continue to increase one st at each edge, every other row, 6 times; then increase every fourth row, 6 times: 58 sts.

sleeve

Work even until Sleeve measures approximately 19½" (49.5 cm) from beginning ch.

Finish off.

finishing

Place a marker at each edge of Sleeve, 1¾" (4.5 cm) down from last row for underarm seam placement. Place a marker at center of last row.

Whipstitch Sleeve seam from wrist edge to markers ***(Figs. 1a & b, page 43)***; do **not** remove edge markers.

Matching Sleeve edge markers to underarm marker and center Sleeve marker to shoulder marker, whipstitch Sleeve to armhole.

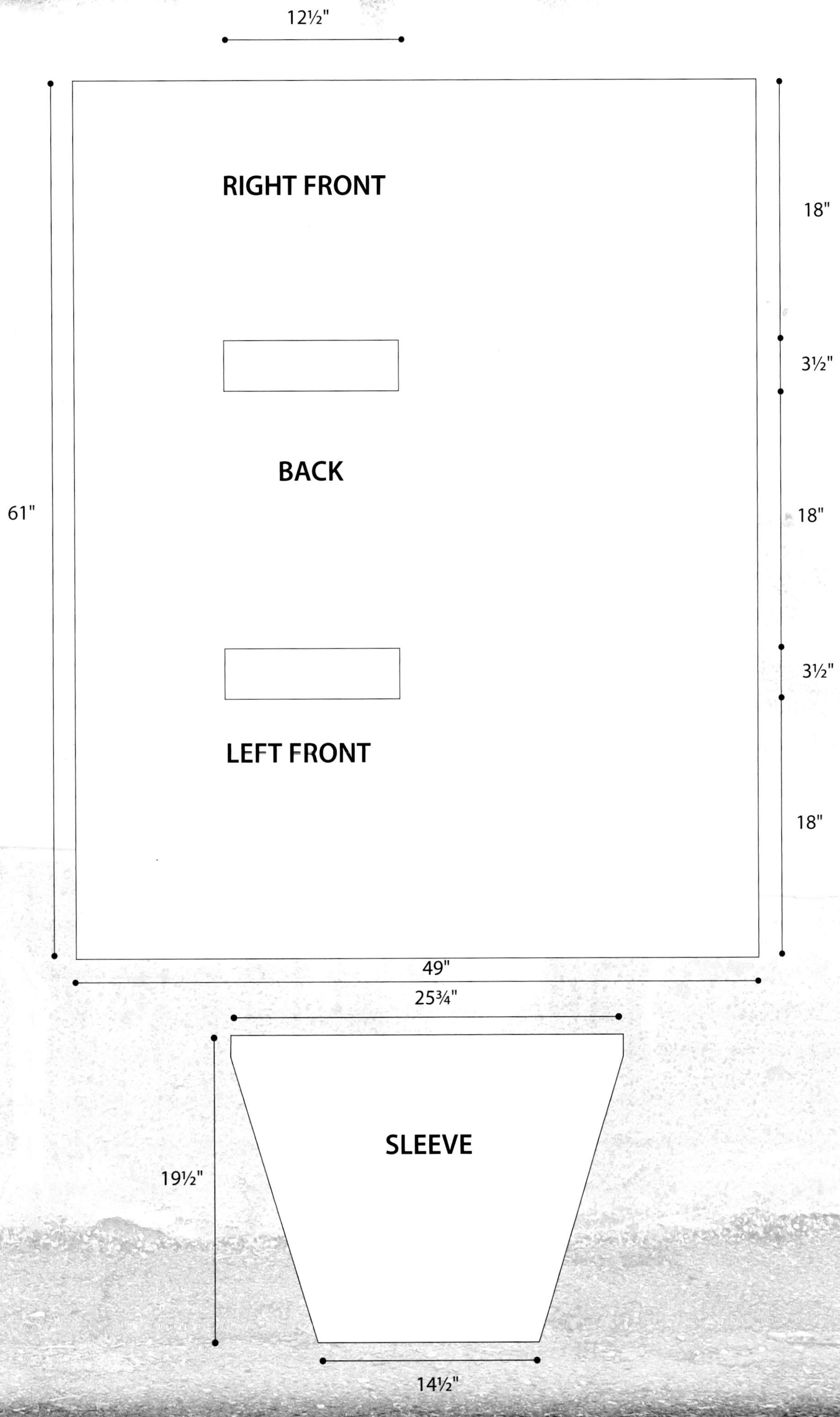
12½"
RIGHT FRONT
18"
3½"
BACK
61"
18"
3½"
LEFT FRONT
18"
49"
25¾"
SLEEVE
19½"
14½"

general instructions

abbreviations

BPdc	Back Post double crochet(s)
ch(s)	chain(s)
cm	centimeters
hdc	half double crochet(s)
dc	double crochet(s)
dc/sc2tog	double crochet/ single crochet 2 together
FPdc	Front Post double crochet(s)
mm	millimeters
sc	single crochet(s)
sc/dc2tog	single crochet/ double crochet 2 together
sp(s)	space(s)
st(s)	stitch(es)
YO	yarn over

symbols & terms

( ) or **[ ]** — work enclosed instructions **as many** times as specified by the number immediately following **or** work all enclosed instructions in the stitch or space indicated **or** contains explanatory remarks.

colon (:) — the number(s) given after a colon at the end of a row or round denote(s) the number of stitches or spaces you should have on that row or round.

work even — work without increasing or decreasing in the established pattern.

CROCHET TERMINOLOGY		
UNITED STATES		INTERNATIONAL
slip stitch (slip st)	=	single crochet (sc)
single crochet (sc)	=	double crochet (dc)
half double crochet (hdc)	=	half treble crochet (htr)
double crochet (dc)	=	treble crochet (tr)
treble crochet (tr)	=	double treble crochet (dtr)
double treble crochet (dtr)	=	triple treble crochet (ttr)
triple treble crochet (tr tr)	=	quadruple treble crochet (qtr)
skip	=	miss

Yarn Weight Symbol & Names	LACE 0	SUPER FINE 1	FINE 2	LIGHT 3	MEDIUM 4	BULKY 5	SUPER BULKY 6	JUMBO 7
Type of Yarns in Category	Fingering, size 10 crochet thread	Sock, Fingering, Baby	Sport, Baby	DK, Light Worsted	Worsted, Afghan, Aran	Chunky, Craft, Rug	Super Bulky, Roving	Jumbo, Roving
Crochet Gauge* Ranges in Single Crochet to 4" (10 cm)	32-42 sts**	21-32 sts	16-20 sts	12-17 sts	11-14 sts	8-11 sts	6-9 sts	5 sts and fewer
Advised Hook Size Range	Steel*** 6 to 8, Regular hook B-1	B-1 to E-4	E-4 to 7	7 to I-9	I-9 to K-10½	K-10½ to M/N-13	M/N-13 to Q	Q and larger

*GUIDELINES ONLY: The chart above reflects the most commonly used gauges and hook sizes for specific yarn categories.

** Lace weight yarns are usually crocheted with larger hooks to create lacy openwork patterns. Accordingly, a gauge range is difficult to determine. Always follow the gauge stated in your pattern.

*** Steel crochet hooks are sized differently from regular hooks–the higher the number, the smaller the hook, which is the reverse of regular hook sizing.

●○○○ **BASIC**	Projects using basic stitches. May include basic increases and decreases.
●●○○ **EASY**	Projects may include simple stitch patterns, color work, and/or shaping.
●●●○ **INTERMEDIATE**	Projects may include involved stitch patterns, color work, and/or shaping.
●●●● **COMPLEX**	Projects may include complex stitch patterns, color work, and/or shaping using a variety of techniques and stitches simultaneously.

CROCHET HOOKS

U.S.	B-1	C-2	D-3	E-4	F-5	G-6	7	H-8	I-9	J-10	K-10½	L-11	M/N-13	N/P-15	P/Q	Q	S
Metric - mm	2.25	2.75	3.25	3.5	3.75	4	4.5	5	5.5	6	6.5	8	9	10	15	16	19

gauge

Exact gauge is **essential** for proper fit. Before beginning your project, make the sample swatch given in the individual instructions in the yarn and hook specified. After completing the swatch, measure it, counting your stitches and rows carefully. If your swatch is larger or smaller than specified, **make another, changing hook size to get the correct gauge**. Keep trying until you find the size hook that will give you the specified gauge. Once proper gauge is obtained, measure width of piece approximately every 3" (7.5 cm) to be sure gauge remains consistent.

zeros

To consolidate the length of an involved pattern, zeros are sometimes used so that all sizes can be combined. For example, increase one st at each edge, every other row, {0-0}{0-1-6} time(s) means the first 3 sizes would not increase, the fourth size would increase once, and the largest size would increase 6 times.

whipstitch

With **wrong** sides together, sew through both pieces once to secure the beginning of the seam, leaving an ample yarn end to weave in later. Insert the needle from **right** to **left** through two strands of each stitch on **both** pieces *(Fig. 1a)* **or** through ends of rows *(Fig. 1b)*. Bring the needle around and insert it from **right** to **left** through the next strands on both pieces.

Repeat along the edge, being careful to match stitches and rows.

Fig. 1a

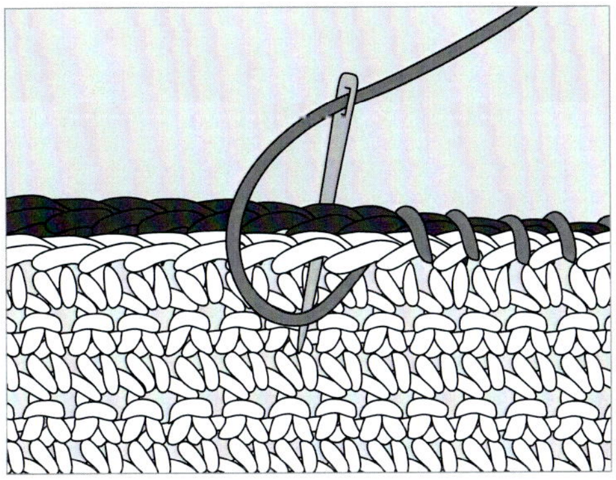

Fig. 1b

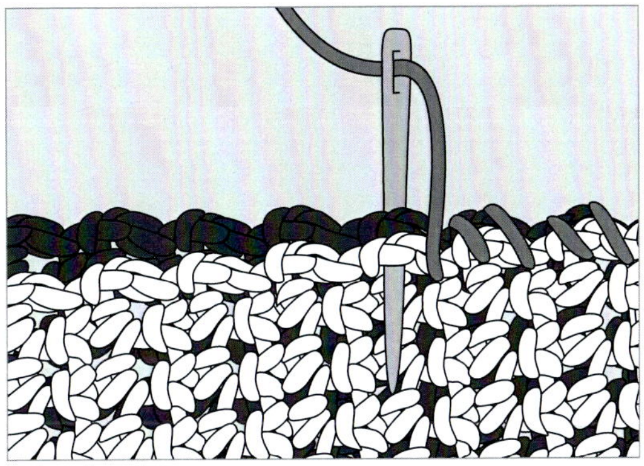

yarn information

The garments in this book were made using Medium or Bulky Weight yarn. Any brand of the specified weight of yarn may be used. It is best to refer to the yardage/meters when determining how many balls or skeins to purchase. Remember, to arrive at the finished size, it is the GAUGE/TENSION that is important, not the brand of yarn.

For your convenience, listed below are the yarns used to create our photography models. Because yarn manufacturers make frequent changes in their product lines, you may sometimes find it necessary to use a substitute yarn or to search for the discontinued product at alternate suppliers (locally or online).

STRIPED TUNIC
Red Heart® Dreamy™
Off White - #8311 Ivory
Grey - #8341 Grey

MISTY HOODIE
Red Heart® Unforgettable™
#3944 Bistro

BLACK & STRAPPY
Lion's Pride® Woolspun®
#153 Black

SLOUCHY PULLOVER
Lion Brand® Jeans®
#109 Stonewash

PLAYFUL PONCHO
Lion Brand® Jeans®
#105 Faded

UNCONSTRUCTED JACKET
Lion Brand® Wool-Ease®
#402 Wheat

Melissa Leapman

With more than 800 knit and crochet designs in print, Melissa Leapman is one of the most widely published American designers working today.

She began her design career by freelancing for leading ready-to-wear design houses in New York City. She also created designs to help top yarn companies promote their new and existing yarns each season. Her ability to quickly develop fully envisioned garments put her skills in great demand.

Through the years, Leisure Arts has published more than 40 books of Melissa's fabulous designs. Melissa is also the host of several Leisure Arts DVDs in the best-selling teach-yourself series, *"I Can't Believe I'm Knitting"* and *"I Can't Believe I'm Crocheting."*

Nationally, her designs have been featured in numerous magazines, and her workshops on knitting and crochet are consistently popular with crafters of all skill levels. She has taught at major events such as STITCHES, Vogue Knitting LIVE, and The Knitting Guild Association conferences, as well as at hundreds of yarn shops and local guild events across the country.

Look for other Leisure Arts books featuring Melissa's designs at www.leisurearts.com/meet-the-designers/melissa-leapman.html.

We have made every effort to ensure that these instructions are accurate and complete. We cannot, however, be responsible for human error, typographical mistakes, or variations in individual work.

Garments made and instructions tested by Raymelle Greening, Leticia McAllister, Barbara Schou, and Kay Shultz.

Production Team: Instructional/Technical Editor - Linda A. Daley; Senior Graphic Artist - Lora Puls; Graphic Artist - Shell Stoll; Photo Stylist - Lori Wenger; and Photographer - Jason Masters.

Made in U.S.A.